From Dorset With Love

From Dorset With Love

An evocative view of Dorset by BOB CROXFORD

*"As to the modern Dorſetſhire gentry, they are very much like
the ſoil they live on, open, free, and generous; full of life
and ſpirit; good artiſts and mechanics in general, and their
heads well turned to trade and merchandize; they are gay and
polite at the ſame time, very ſtudious and lovers of ſcience in
every ſhape; and conſequently no great friends to
ſuperſtition. ——- In ſhort, you no where breathe a finer air,
nor converſe with a better ſet of people."*

1768

Published by ATMOSPHERE

FROM DORSET WITH LOVE

Photographs Copyright Bob Croxford 1996

Text copyright Bob Croxford 1996

(except where separately acknowledged).

Design copyright Ann Butcher and Atmosphere

Anthology compilation copyright Bob Croxford

Second Impression 1999

First published by ATMOSPHERE in 1996

Willis Vean

Mullion

Helston Cornwall TR12 7DF

TEL: 01326 240180

FAX: 01326 240900

ISBN 0 9521850 3 2

Designed by Ann Butcher

Origination by Scantec Repro, Cornwall

Printed and bound in Italy by L.E.G.O. Vicenza

Also by BOB CROXFORD

FROM CORNWALL WITH LOVE   ISBN 09521850 0 8

FROM DEVON WITH LOVE   ISBN 09521850 1 6

FROM BATH WITH LOVE   ISBN 09521850 2 4

FROM THE COTSWOLDS WITH LOVE   ISBN 09521850 4 0

COVER PICTURE: Coast at Durdle Door

CONTENTS

INTRODUCTION

Dorset is a tiny county. From Portland Bill nearly the entire coastline from Lyme Regis to Durlston Head can be seen. From a ridge near Abbotsbury you can see a fair proportion of the interior, as well as almost the entire coastline. Residents of Lyme Regis think nothing of driving across the county to see a concert in Bournemouth.

But Dorset is a county of contrasts in a remarkably small area. The underlying geology creates a rich and varied coastline. Downs and heaths, valleys and hills, streams and rivers all add to a rich landscape. Dorset delights in difference and novelty. The metropolis of Poole and Bournemouth seems so big compared with small hamlets just a few miles away.

History has also shaped and influenced the county. Early peoples had a sophisticated social fabric. They built settlements on Hambledon and Eggardon Hills, both are superbly situated iron age hillforts. Before that time the neolithic people built henge monuments, standing stones and tumuli. Of course we could go back to the time of the Dinosaurs who left footprints on the Isle of Purbeck. Some will prefer to mention the Jurassic cliffs near Lyme and Charmouth, where fossils abound.

The Romans came more recently, building roads, towns and villas. Danes, Saxons and Normans all make an entry in the pageant.

Dividing Dorset into logical chapters depends on how one views the place. A geologist sees it in terms of what sits invisibly under the grass, woodland and heath. A botanist spots the difference in the plants which depend on the geology below. An entomologist notes the different plants which are favoured by butterflies and beetles.

Non specialists will simply see the landscape around them. A resident of Shaftesbury would see things differently to a person from Weymouth. I have started with Lyme Regis and ended with Corfe Castle. Both are good bits. When I came to the places in between, I imagined this book a bit like an overfilled egg-mayonnaise sandwich. So many good pictures. So many pretty villages, beautiful landscapes, dramatic seascapes, tranquil valleys, picturesque harbours, ruined castles, thatched cottages, historic places, elegant towns,…. all squeezing to get in! If your favourite place fell out onto the editor's lap, I apologize.

This is not a catalogue. I have tried to make this book evocative of Dorset.

The photographs are accompanied by a collection of writings on the County. In compiling this anthology I have tried to add a counterpoint to the images rather than a series of captions. The pictures do not illustrate the captions, nor the captions the pictures.

Literature, poetry, history and travel have all produced a plethora of good books. My selection is chosen to show the variety of big and small events, funny and serious issues and greater and lesser characters.

Dorset Apple Cake >

THE WEST

From Exeter to Weymouth there are few harbours. In the days of sail Chesil Beach was a graveyard for ships. West Bay near Bridport was racked by feuding of a feudal kind. From early times, until the coming of the modern road surface, transport was on the high and dry downland. Narrow wagons, built for the terrain, carried goods to and fro.

Lyme Regis barely scrapes into Dorset. The tentacles of Devon seem to be reaching out to engulf this pearl of heritage and beauty. With its steep hills down to the sea, it is a wonder that Lyme developed as a town at all. Much is made of the difficulties of pack-horses taking goods to and from the harbour. In the period of Lyme's growth in the 12th century, horses were commonly used for the carriage of goods, due to the poor state of the trackways and roads.

In a decisive move to improve the infrastructure the Cobb was built in about 1250. It provided shelter for local fishing boats as well as cargo ships. At first the Cobb was simply a breakwater but later additions gave Lyme a fully functioning harbour.

Just as Lyme went into decline as a port, in the late 18th century, it became famous for sea-bathing. The assembly rooms became a fashionable place for Society to meet. Jane Austen was a visitor.

The cliffs either side of Lyme Regis are extremely unstable and land-slips frequently occur. The sedimentation occurred in the Mesolithic and Jurassic periods. When slips occur fossils of long-dead creatures are exposed. A local girl, Mary Anning, found the first complete ichthyosaur skeleton in 1810. At the time she was eleven years old. She continued to collect fossils and became well known throughout Europe. She once told a crowned king of Saxony that she was more well known in Europe than he was!

East from Lyme Regis are a series of cliffs with sheltered valleys in between. Most dramatic of these is Golden Cap. At over 190 metres high, it is the highest cliff on the south coast.

Bridport is a fine, old market town built on a similar plan to Dorchester. Its chief industry was rope making. The rich soil of Marshwood Vale was suitable for the growing of hemp and flax. At a time when the British Navy depended on sailing ships with extensive rigging, rope was of strategic importance.

The farmers grew rich cultivating the crop. The rope makers wound up rich by turning it into rope and nets. The boatmen at West Bay made a profit delivering the rope direct to the ships in Lyme Bay. Everything went to make Bridport a prosperous little town. Unfortunately, the wealth rarely reached West Bay. Accounts through the ages tell of fights between fishermen and farmers. The result is that West Bay is a bit like "Bridport-by-the-Sea". It was only with great difficulty that the harbour was built, and kept open against the shifting shingle.

The strata in Burton Cliffs, just east of West Bay, show the start of a limestone layer that runs through England, all the way to Yorkshire.

Away from the coast, the downs of West Dorset are an almost forgotten land. Hills surmounted by iron-age hill-forts, rolling green valleys and narrow country lanes make a typical English landscape. Perhaps the lanes are too narrow for modern drivers or perhaps the idea of an English holiday is to be beside the sea.

A lot of people dream of living at the seaside. With Abbotsbury you are close but at the same time tantalizingly far away. Chesil Beach is a long strip of shingle which contains a lagoon of brackish water. Abbotsbury is on one side of the lagoon, the sea on the other side of the shingle. The pebbles which comprise Chesil Beach are graded, by the sea, into different sizes. The smaller ones are at the Abbotsbury end. In the days of sailing vessels Chesil had a fearsome reputation. Many boats were driven onto the beach where the fierce undertow could carry away sailors yards away from the shore. The old cottages of the village have a very yellow colour which is attributed to the local quarry. Most of the stone came from the old monastery which had yellowed with age. The abbey barn, which was originally 270 feet long, is a testament to the wealth of the monks. St Catherine's Chapel, the 14th century landmark above Abbotsbury stands on a hill of sculpted strip lynchets, early signs of cultivation. This chapel escaped destruction because it made a very useful navigation aid for sailors.

Chesil Beach is a fifteen mile bank of shingle enclosing a lagoon known as the Fleet. As the pebbles are very difficult to walk on the beach is rarely visited. Its isolation make it a haven for wild birds most famously the large number of swans which congregate at Abbotsbury. Duck decoys have been used at Abbotsbury for centuries. The monks used the swannery as a source of food. They ate the swans.

Lyme Regis >

There was too much wind to make the high part of the new Cobb pleasant for the ladies, and they agreed to get down the steps to the lower; and all were contented to pass quietly and carefully down the steep flight, excepting Louisa: she must be jumped down them by Captain Wentworth. In all their walks he had had to jump her from the stiles; the sensation was delightful to her. The hardness of the pavement for her feet made him less willing upon the present occasion; he did it however. She was safely down, and instantly to show her enjoyment, ran up the steps to be jumped down again. He advised her against it, thought the jar too great; but no, he reasoned and talked in vain; she smiled and said, "I am determined I will". He put out his hands; she was too precipitate by half a second; she fell on the pavement on the lower Cobb, and was taken up lifeless!

There was no wound, no blood, no visible bruise; but her eyes were closed, she breathed not, her face was like death. The horror of that moment to all who stood around!

JANE AUSTEN 1818

The morning, when Sam drew the curtains, flooded in upon Charles as Mrs Poulteney - then still audibly asleep - would have wished paradise to flood in upon her, after a suitably solemn pause, when she died. A dozen times or so a year the climate of the mild Dorset coast yields such days - not just agreeably mild out-of-season days, but ravishing fragments of Mediterranean warmth and luminosity. Nature goes a little mad then. Spiders that should be hibernating run over the baking November rocks; blackbirds sing in December, primroses rush out in January; and March mimics June.

JOHN FOWLES 1969

< *Lyme Regis from the air*
Lyme Harbour at dawn >

*T*his Evening betwixt 7 & 8 of ye Clock there came in great Shipp into ye Rode of Lyme not showing any Cullors... She filled five great Boats full of men, & they speeded behinde ye Cobb, and soe Landed them to the Weftward of ye Towne...at leaft three hundred men, the Duke of Monmouth in ye head of them, soe yt they became Mafters of ye Towne.

GREGORY ALFORD *(Mayor of Lyme)* 11th June 1685

*A*t such conjunctures a short time produces a great change, and now an insurrection had begun. All things were in confusion. He delivered the powder to two of the magistrates, going towards his house, Dassell saw the enemy, as he styles the party, marching, and many townsmen joining, and others rejoicing and crying out, "A Monmouth! a Monmouth! - the Protestant religion!"

GEORGE ROBERTS 1844

Cannon on the harbour wall >

< Storm at Lyme Regis

Charles had already visited what was perhaps the most famous shop in the Lyme of those days - the Old Fossil Shop, founded by the remarkable Mary Anning, a woman without formal education but with a genius for discovering good - and on many occasions then unclassified - specimens. She was the first person to see the bones of **Ichthyosaurus platyodon**; *and one of the meanest disgraces of British palaeontology is that although many scientists of the day gratefully used her finds to establish their own reputation, not one native type bears the specific* **anningii**.

JOHN FOWLES 1969

Customers squeeze their way past one another round the jam-packed tables and shelves of the Fossil Shop. You don't have to buy anything, but your will must be of iron if you can leave this treasure cave empty-handed. Apart from the fossils and lumps of deeply coloured crystalline rock on sale for any sum between £1 and upwards of £100, there's a large display of unsaleable items - too big, too rare - such as ammonites three feet across, split in half and polished, their internal segments filled with sparkling crystallized sand. There are enormous towers of amethyst; ordinary-looking pebbles known as geodes whose hollow hearts are encrusted with gem-like crystals; tiny trilobites like marine woodlice, smaller than your little fingernail. Here Lyme cheerfully, but not aggressively, sets about cashing in on the good fortune lying under its cliffs.

< Fossil Beach, Charmouth
Golden Cap >

CHRISTOPHER SOMERVILLE 1989

*T*he greatest inconvenience we suffer here is in being so far from the post office; with respect to household conveniences we do very well, as the butcher coming from Cruikhern brings us every thing we want. With respect to letters we are however, more independent than most people as William is so good a walker, and I too have walked over twice to Crewkhern to make purchases.

DOROTHY WORDSWORTH 30th November 1795

*T*he county of Dorset is small, but is yet so varied in its configuration as to present an epitome of the scenery of Southern England. It is a land of moods and changes that knows no monotony, and is indeed so full of hills and dales that there is scarcely a level road within its confines, save by the banks of streams.

FREDERICK TREVES May 1906

< View below Pilsdon Pen
Country Letter Box >

*D*ine at Bridport, a very neat town, whoſe principal ſtreet is remarkably ſpacious, wellbuilt, and paved; about the middle ſtands an excellent new market houſe, with good rooms over it for all public purpoſes, only finished this year.

REV S SHAW 1788

*I*ts ſoil is ſo particular, that it yields hemp to much greater perfection than in any other county; nay, we may add, than in any other county throughout the kingdom of England. And as a demonſtration of the truth of it, this town, tho' in all other reſpects inconſiderable enough, was heretofore ſo famous for making ropes and cables for ſhips, that it was provided by a ſpecial law, which was appointed to continue for a ſtated time, that ſuch tackle as ſhould be appropriated to the ſervice of the Engliſh navy, ſhould be made no where elſe...

RURAL ELEGANCE 1768

West Bay >
< Burton Cliffs

St. Catherine, St. Catherine, oh lend me thine aid,

And grant that I niver may die an wold maid.

A husband, St. Catherine,

A good one St. Catherine;

But arn-a-one better than

Narn-a-one, St. Catherine.

Sweet St. Catherine,

A husband, St. Catherine

Handsome, St. Catherine,

Rich, St. Catherine,

Soon, St. Catherine.

ANON

Twix' the Lizard and Dover

We hand the stuff over,

Though I may not inform how we do it, and when.

But a light on each quarter

Low down on the water

Is well understood by poor honest men!

RUDYARD KIPLING 1865 -1936

St. Catherine's Chapel and The Fleet >
< Abbotsbury

*O*ur village lies near the centre of Moonfleet Bay, a great bight twenty miles across, and a death-trap to up-channel sailors in a south-westerly gale. For with that wind blowing strong from south, if you cannot double the Snout, you must most surely come ashore; and many a good ship failing to round that point has beat up and down the bay all day, but come to beach in the evening. And once on the beach, the sea has little mercy, for the water is deep right in, and the waves curl over full on the pebbles with a weight no timbers can withstand. Then if poor fellows try to save themselves, there is a deadly under-tow or rush back of the water, which sucks them off their legs, and carries them again under the thundering waves. It is that back-suck of the pebbles that you may hear for miles inland, even at Dorchester, on still nights long after the winds that caused it have sunk, and which makes people turn in their beds, and thank God they are not fighting with the sea on Moonfleet beach.

JOHN MEADE-FALKNER 1898

Chesil Beach from Portland >
< A swan on the Fleet

WEYMOUTH AND PORTLAND

In mediaeval times there were two settlements, and two separate harbours, on either side of the River Wey. One was large and called Melcombe Regis. The other settlement, on the south side of the river was small and called Weymouth. As ports they were both rivals for the tolls, dues and trade that cargo ships brought. When the two settlements merged in 1571 they took the name Weymouth although Melcombe Regis was far larger. Perhaps the good burghers of Melcombe Regis were trying to live down their poor reputation. The Black Death arrived, in England, through their harbour.

As larger transatlantic boats docked at bigger, more convenient ports the town went into decline. This was reversed by the new craze for sea bathing in the mid 18th century. George III made the resort fashionable between 1780 and 1850. Bathing machines on wheels were pulled down the beach at low tide. Sea bathing was taken seriously as a health benefit. Attendants in the bathing machines explained the type and length of the immersion required. Although bathing was considered healthy, over-immersion was considered injurious to the brain. When George III appeared from his bathing machine and entered the water a brass band played "God save the King". Perhaps he stayed in the water too long. He soon had a reputation for madness.

This fashionable period brought the town many elegant buildings. In 1857 the railway arrived and the days of mass tourism began. The trains first brought the upper middle classes. Then, after the Boer War, it was the turn of the self made tradesmen from England's industrial belt. After the Second World War many of the working class had a holiday for the first time.

Portland would be an island, but for the Chesil Bank. The 15 mile long strip of shingle contains the Fleet to make it a lagoon. It then swings out to sea and joins with the chunk of limestone turning it into a peninsula. Until a road was built visitors went to Portland by boat. Try walking on the smooth pebbles for a few miles and you'll see why.

The stone is particularly favoured because of its pale, even colour. Quarries are everywhere. Portland is mostly famous for what isn't there! Wren used Portland stone for his "new" Cathedral, St. Paul's. Many other fine buildings also came from Portland. Henry Moore became famous for carving holes in the stuff.

The immense harbour between Weymouth and Portland was built between 1847 and 1872. The labour for the work was provided by inmates at Portland Prison. In fact the gaol was finished at the same time as work on the harbour wall began. It was a typical victorian solution. Build a prison on a lump of stone. Sentence a lot of men to prison for minor offences like stealing a loaf of bread. Give them all heavy hammers and in the time it takes to say "prison reform trust" you have enough stone to build an immense sea defence. When Albert, Prince of Wales opened the breakwater in 1872 I bet they didn't invite many convicts.

Despite its heavy and oppressive industrial past, Portland and its small villages have a certain dramatic quality. The great engineer John Smeaton describes the interesting social curcumstances which prevailed in 18th century.

"Our people here," said Mr Roper, "as they are bred up to hard labour, are very early in a condition to marry and provide for a family; they intermarry with one another, very rarely going to the main land to seek a wife; and it has been the custom of the island, from time immemorial, that they never marry till the woman is pregnant." "But pray," says I, "does not this subject you to a great number of bastards?" "None at all," replies Roper, "for, previous to my arrival here, there was but one child on record of the Parish register that had been born a bastard in the compass of 150 years. The mode of courtship here is, that a young woman never admits of the serious addresses of a young man but on supposition of a thorough probation. When she becomes with child, she tells her mother, the mother tells her father; her father tells his father; and he tells his son, that it is then proper time to be married. "But suppose, Mr Roper, she does not prove with child, what happens then; do they live together without marriage; or, if they separate, is not this such an imputation upon her as to prevent her getting another suitor?" "The case is thus managed," answered my friend, "if the woman does not prove with child, after a competent time of courtship, they conclude they are not destined by Providence for each other; they therefore separate; and as it is an established maxim, which the Portland women observe with great strictness, never to admit a plurality of lover at any one time, their honour is in no ways tarnished, she just as soon gets another suitor as if she had been left a widow, or that nothing had ever happened but that she remained an immaculate virgin."

Portland slopes, like a wedge of cheese, towards the south. The lighthouse at the tip was built in 1905. The earlier lighthouse is now used as an observatory to count migrating birds.

Weymouth Harbour >

*W*EYMOUTH, the view of which, as you approach it, is very fine. The profpect confifts of the town, fituated in a low, but agreeable fpot, commanding at the fame time the fea, and a diftant view of the Ifle of Portland. Weymouth is a little, narrow, dirty place, ill-paved, and irregulary built. The new ftreet, called the Efplanade, is well fituated, and facing the fea, has a handfome appearance. It refembles that part of Brighton which wears the fame afpect. Was it not for its bathing place, and the late vifits of the King, few would refort to Weymouth for the pleafure it affords. It has, perhaps, the fineft fhore for bathing in the whole world. A fine clear fea, with a beautiful carpet of white fand gradually declining, invites even the moft timid to the luxury of the water.

E D CLARKE 1791

The Mayor advancing in a common way, to take the Queen's hand, as he might that of any lady mayoress, Colonel Gwynn, who stood by, whispered: "You must kneel, sir!" He found, however, that he took no notice of this hint, but kissed the Queen's hand erect. As he passed him, in his way back, the Colonel said: "You should have knelt, sir!"
"Sir," answered the poor Mayor "I cannot."
"Everybody does, sir"
"Sir - I have a wooden leg!"
Poor man! Such a surprise! And such an excuse no one could dispute.

FANNY BURNEY   1798

< Weymouth Harbour
The Clocktower >

*T*he King's bathing machine is in the form of an oblong at its base, and painted white, with the panels blue and red cornices, but is destitute of lining. The outside, at the top, forms a semicircle, on the extremity of which stands upon a pole, of about two feet in length, the crown; and on the other, the British flag, on a pole, or standard, of about ten feet high; on the front is painted the King's arms.

FANNY BURNEY 1798

*T*he Sea lost nothing of the swallowing identity of its great outer mass of waters in the emphatic, individual character of each particular wave. Each wave, as it rolled in upon the high-pebbled beach, was an epitome of the whole body of the sea, and carried with it all the vast mysterious quality of the earth's ancient antagonist.

JOHN COWPER POWYS 1934

Pulpit Rock >
< Weymouth Sands

I will go forth a wanderer on the earth,
A shadowy thing, and as I wander on
No human ear shall ever hear my voice,
No human dwelling ever give me food
Or sleep or rest, and all the uncertain way
Shall be as darkness to me, as a waste
Unnamed by man! and I will wander on
Living by mere intensity of thought,
A thing by pain and thought compelled to live,
Yet loathing life, till heaven in mercy strike me
With blank forgetfulness - that I may die.

WILLIAM WORDSWORTH 1797

*T*he ſoil of Portland affords rather an unpleaſing aſpect. With hardly a mark of fertility, or the grateful features of wood and paſture, the whole ſpot appears bleak and barren. The poor, though well provided for in other reſpects, experience a great ſcarcity of fuel. Neceſſity has, however, taught them to ſubſtitute the dung of cattle in its ſtead. They apply it wet to the walls, and the ſides of their houſes, where it adheres until it is fit for uſe, when they collect it together, and burn it, as the poor in other parts of England conſume their peat.

E D CLARKE 1791

Portland Lighthouse >
< Portland Bill from the air

DORCHESTER AND THE CENTRE

Dorchester is the county town of Dorset. It still has the feel of a provincial market town. Large enough to be the natural centre for all the villages around, it is small enough to be on a pleasant human scale. Dorchester would be just a sleepy market town but for three things which make it famous.

Maiden Castle is probably the best known hill-fort in England. Starting with a neolithic enclosure it has been an area of human activity for thousands of years. In the Iron Age the Castle was extended several times. In the Late Iron Age two extra ramparts were added. The defences at the entrances were also strengthened. The sheer scale and size of these works indicate how important the site was in pre-historic times. The Romans dramatically captured the castle in 43 or 44 AD. A few years later the Roman settlement of *Durnovaria*, later Dorchester, was established in parallel with further work at Maiden Castle. The Romans established a road network which made it a centre for communications.

The second thing to make Dorchester famous was the Assize Court of Judge Jeffries, "The Hanging Judge". After the Duke of Monmouth's rebellion many who had joined him, and a few who had not, were tried and executed. The methods Jeffries took to get convictions were one of the most shameful in the history of English justice.

The third thing to make the town famous was when the local writer, Thomas Hardy, re-named the town Casterbridge.

A short way outside the village of

Winterbourne Abbas stands a group of megalithic stones. Known locally as Nine Stones it dates from early bronze age. Despite the busy main road close by, peace and calmness envelope one as soon as you step near to the stones.

The compact village of Cerne Abbas has become justly famous for its beauty. Fine old houses line the streets and a pub pretends to be a bit of forest. It is a hill just outside the village that makes it more famous still. The Cerne Abbas Giant is a giant chalk figure cut into the hillside. Controversy rages over the date and use of the proud man. A likely explanation is that the figure was British from just before the Roman invasion. When the Romans arrived they adapted many of the local gods to fit with their own deities. Perhaps the Cerne Giant became a local Hercules. He strides naked across the hill brandishing a club. The chalk is scoured clean occasionally and it was during one of these renovations that the penis joined his navel. This made him even ruder than before.

The Sycamore Tree in the centre of Tolpuddle was the sheltered meeting place of the Tolpuddle Martyrs. It was here that the six men met to plan the idea of a union to defend their rights. Their farmer employers wanted them to accept a drop of two shillings a week in wages. In these days a woman's wages were barely two shillings per week). Tolpuddle was to become the virtual birthplace of Trade Unionism. Found guilty of mutiny at a trial in Dorchester, George Loveless, one of the six, was sent to Tasmania and the others to Sydney, Australia. The men

worked with chain gangs, on the roads and on government farms, but few could have reckoned on the support these six people had gathered in their native land. Mass meetings, petitions and rallies were organised and finally in 1836 the campaigners obtained a full and free pardon for the men. The great sycamore on the green is probably the very tree under which the men met to plan their union.

Town, or village, planning existed in the 18th century, but for different reasons than today. Lord Milton built his grand house next to the Abbey church at Milton Abbas in 1774. The monastery had long departed but a thriving village had grown up around the abbey buildings. Lord Milton didn't like the idea of having the villagers as his close neighbours. The solution was to build another village around the corner and out of sight. The village of Milton Abbas has not changed since it was built except to have a church in 1786. The almshouses were built from material taken from the old village. It is now mostly a commuter village but there are enough local children to have a lively nursery school in the almshouse hall.

In every Dorset valley runs a stream or river. The rivers of Dorset are many. So, also, are the bridges. River crossings were important to the development of towns and villages. To build a bridge was a massive undertaking in mediaeval times. Often an abbey or church would finance the construction in return for tolls charged to every user. Crawford Bridge at Spetisbury is a good example of a large stone bridge which still includes parts which are mediaeval.

One of Dorset's many elegant bridges crosses

the River Stour at Blandford Forum. The river crossing made the town a natural site for a market. It is a centre for the rich agricultural economy around it. The town was destroyed by fire in 1731. When the town was rebuilt the classical principles of the Georgian style were the fashion. Blandford Forum was sufficiently rich to build many fine houses. Credit should go to local builders, architects and developers, the brothers William and John Bastard.

Dorset is well endowed with ancient sites; Megalithic stone monuments, henges, tumuli, camps, barrows, ditches and forts. The iron age hillfort of Badbury Rings is one of the best in the country. Its concentric ramparts were much steeper when it was in use. The site is sufficiently raised for the Romans to use it when building two nearby roads.

A circle of a different kind, and much older, is to be found at Knowlton. Knowlton Ring is a neolithic henge which was probably used as a sacred site. It lies to the east of a magnificent avenue of trees. The trees were planted by the Kingston Lacy estate. In total there are 365 beech trees. One for every day of the year. Don't try counting them now. The National Trust has added another row to ensure that the avenue lasts another few hundred years.

Dorchester High Street >

Erect a gallows in the most public place of your city to hang the rebels on; provide halters to hang them with, sufficient amount of faggots to burn the bowels of the traitors, and a furnace and cauldron to boil their heads and quarters, and salt to boil therewith, half a bushel for each traitor, and tar to tar them with, and a sufficient number of spears and poles to fix their heads and quarters. You are also to provide an axe and cleaver for quartering the said rebels.

I this day began with the trial of the rebels at Dorchester, and have despatched ninety-eight.....

JUDGE JEFFRIES 1685

Maiden Castle from the air >
< Dorchester

DORSET

Rime Intrinsica, Fontmell Magna, Sturminster Newton and Melbury Bubb,
Whist upon whist upon whist upon whist drive, in Institute, Legion and Social Club.
Horny hands that hold the aces which this morning held the plough -
While Tranter Reuben, T.S.Eliot, H.G.Wells and Edith Sitwell

lie in Mellstock Churchyard now.

Lord's Day bells from Bingham's Melcombe, Iwerne Minster, Shroton, Plush,
Down the grass between the beeches, mellow in the evening hush.
Gloved the hands that hold the hymn-book, which this morning milked the cow -
While Tranter Reuben, Mary Borden, Brian Howard and Harold Acton

lie in Mellstock Churchyard now.

Light's abode, celestial Salem! Lamps of evening, smelling strong,
Gleaming on the pitch-pine, waiting, almost empty evensong:
From the aisles each window smiles on grave and grass and yew-tree bough -
While Tranter Reuben, Gordon Selfridge, Edna Best and Thomas Hardy

lie in Mellstock Churchyard now.

JOHN BETJEMAN   1958

He seemed perfectly aware of everything; in no
doubt or hesitation; having made up his mind;
and being delivered of all his work, so that he
was in no doubt about that either. He was not
interested much in his novels, or in anybody's
novels: took it all easily and naturally. "I never
took long with them" he said. "The longest was
The Dinnasts (so Pronounced). Yes; and that took
me six years; but not working all the time."

VIRGINIA WOOLFE   July 25th 1926

< Thomas Hardy's birthplace cottage
Thomas Hardy Statue, Dorchester >

However, the church is no match for the public house, and dinner and drink soon make too many of the members heedless of the exhortation, and so, "stark man with pweison stuff," the evening of a club-day presents a sad scene in many a cottage home, for drink is the fiend that misleads men in Dorsetshire as everywhere else. Unhappily, custom favours its temptation, labourers receiving in some cases cider as part of their wages. No doubt both masters and men are under the belief that it helps them to work better.

RICHARD HEATH 1893

In the liquor line Loveday laid in an ample barrel of Dorchester strong beer.... It was of the most beautiful colour that the eye of an artist in beer could desire; full in body, yet brisk as a volcano; piquant, yet without a twang; luminous as an autumn sunset; free from streakiness of taste; but, finally, rather heady.

THOMAS HARDY 1840 - 1928

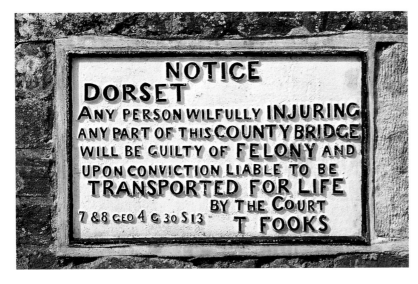

Dorset Pub >
< Punishment Bridge

*T*here is a tradition, that a giant, who resided hereabout in
former ages, the pest and terror of the adjacent country,
having made an excursion into Blackmore, and regaled himself with
several sheep, retired to this hill, and lay down to sleep. The
country people seized this opportunity, pinioned him down, and
killed him, and then traced out the dimensions of his body, to
perpetuate his memory.

JOHN HUTCHINS 1774

A low ridge of hills ends to the north of the abbey, on the west
side of which is a figure cut in lines by taking out the turf
and showing the white chalk. It is called the Giant and Hele, is
about 150 feet long, a naked figure in a genteel posture, with his
left foot set out; it is a sort of a Pantheon figure. In the right hand
he holds a knotted club; the left hand is held out and open, there
being a bend in the elbow , so that it seems to be Hercules, or
Strength and Fidelity, but it is with such indecent circumstances as
to make one conclude it was also a Priapus. It is to be supposed
that this was an ancient figure of worship, and one would imagine
that the people would not permit the monks to destroy it.

DR RICHARD POCOCKE 1754

< The Cerne Abbas Giant
Nine Stones, Winterbourne Abbas >

Nevertheless poverty and a sensitive heart are no protection against the snares of Satan; on the contrary, it is just because he has a sensitive heart that the Dorset peasant is all the more easily crushed and rendered reckless by adversity. Periods of semi-starvation and wretched cottages drive such natures into vice and practical atheism. At whose door lies the sin?

Is this the practical result of modern social economy? If so it is a system by which the poor get poorer, and the rich richer; a system, the evil effects of which are more manifest in the country than in the town, since it is evident that the small landed proprietor, the small farmer, are every day losing ground, while the great landed proprietor and the large farmer are every day adding to their domains and increasing the acreage of their farms.

RICHARD HEATH 1872

My lord, if we have violated any law, it was not done intentionally; we have injured no man's reputation, character, person or property. We were uniting together to preserve ourselves, our wives and our children, from utter degradation and starvation.

GEORGE LOVELESS 1834

< Thatched Cottages at Cerne Abbas
The Tolpuddle Sycamore Tree >

*H*eavy of gait, stolid of mien, and of indomitable courage,
the Wessex man is a staunch friend and a very mild enemy.
He is a genial fellow and, like Danton, seems to find no use for
hate. He knows that all things done in hate have to be done over
again. Imperturbable to the last ditch, he is rarely shaken into
any exclamation of surprise or wrath.

R. THURSTON HOPKINS 1922

*T*he ladies here do not want the help of assemblies to assist in
match-making; or half-pay officers to run away with their
daughters, and yet I observed that the women do not seem to stick
on hands so much in this country, as in those countries, where
those assemblies are so lately set up; the reason of which I cannot
help saying, if my opinion may bear any weight, is, that the
Dorsetshire ladies are equal in beauty, and may be superior in
reputation. And yet the Dorsetshire ladies, I assure you, are not
nuns, they do not go veiled about streets, or hide themselves when
visited; but a general freedom of conversation, agreeable,
mannerly, kind, and good runs through the whole body of the
gentry of both sexes, mixed with the best of behaviour, and yet
governed by prudence and modesty; such as I no where see better in
all my observation, through the whole isle of Britain.

DANIEL DEFOE 1724

< Milton Abbas
Milton Abbas Almshouse >

The case as it stands is maddening. For a successful painter, sculptor, musician, author, who takes society by storm, it is no drawback, it is sometimes even a romantic recommendation, to hail from outcasts and profligates. But for a clergyman of the Church of England! Cornelius, it is fatal! To succeed in the Church, people must believe in you, first of all, as a gentleman, secondly as a man of means, thirdly as a scholar, fourthly as a preacher, fifthly, perhaps, as a Christian - but always first as a gentleman, with all their heart and soul and strength.

THOMAS HARDY 1840-1928

WAGTAIL AND BABY

*A baby watched a ford, whereto
A wagtail came for drinking;
A blaring bull went wading through,
The wagtail showed no shrinking.*

*A stallion splashed his way across,
The birdie nearly sinking;
He gave his plumes a twitch and toss,
And held his own unblinking.*

*Next saw the baby round the spot
A mongrel slowly slinking;
The wagtail gazed, but faltered not
In dip and sip and prinking.*

*A perfect gentleman then neared;
The wagtail, in a winking,
With terror rose and disappeared;
The baby fell a-thinking.*

THOMAS HARDY   1840-1928

*St. Peter and St.Paul Church, Blandford Forum >
< Blandford Forum from the air*

46

*B*ADBURY is ſituated on a conſiderable eminence, about four miles north-weſt from Winborn, the Vindogladia of Antoninus, to which it appears to have been a ſummer ſtation. It was afterwards occupied, however, by the Saxons. We read of Edward the elder poſting himſelf here, when on the march to puniſh his rebellious kinſman, Ethelward, who had taken Winborn. The Roman road leads to the north-eaſt entrance of this fine encampment, which conſiſts of three ſomewhat oblong ramparts, and the inmoſt part commands a moſt extenſive horizon.

WILLIAM GEORGE MATON 1797

WITCHES AND WITCHCRAFT

Her evil wish that had such pow'r
That she did meake their milk an' eale turn zour,
An' addle all the eggs their vowls did lay;...
The dog got dead-alive an' drowsy,
The cat vell zick an' woulden mousy;
An' everytime the vo'k went up to bed,
They wer a hag-rod till they wer half dead.

     A Witch

WILLIAM BARNES 1801 - 1886

< Badbury Rings
Knowlton Henge >

The three autumn months that followed the school treat became for Wolf, as the days shortened and darkened, like a slowly rising tide that, drawing its mass of waters from distances and gulfs beyond his reach, threatened to leave scant space unsubmerged of the rugged rock front which hitherto he had turned upon the world. Something in the very fall of the leaf, in the slow dissolution of vegetation all about him, made this menace to the integrity of his soul more deadly. He had never realized what the word 'autumn' meant until this Wessex autumn gathered its 'cloudy trophies' about his ways, and stole, with its sweet rank odours, into the very recesses of his being. Each calamitous event that occurred during those deciduous months seemed to be brewed in the oozy vat of vegetation, as if the muddy lanes and the wet hazel-copses - yes! the very earth-mould of Dorset itself-were conspiring with human circumstances.

JOHN COWPER POWYS 1934

< Spetisbury Bridge
Kingston Lacy Avenue >

THE NORTH

From the edge of the escarpment at Shaftesbury one appears to survey the whole of Dorset. Below lies the Blackmore Vale and in the distance the Dorset downland which just hides the sea from view. This hilltop town developed around the site of a nunnery which was endowed by King Alfred in 880. Its site, overlooking Blackmore Vale was presumably chosen for defensive purposes. The wealth of the nunnery increased to become the richest in the country. The immense tithe barn at Bradford on Avon was just one of the collecting places for the nuns' wealth. The dissolution of the monasteries ended a prosperous era for this populous town. Water supply has often been a problem. The town had rights to collect water from Enmore at the foot of the hill but this was sometimes disputed. Shaftesbury's unique situation has bought 20th century expansion. Such is the modern world, its fame now seems to rely on television. Gold Hill was once used in a TV commercial for bread!

The view down Gold Hill is world famous. It is one of the only spots where a landscape photographer can work while sitting down. The enjoyment is made complete with a cup of tea and a slice of Dorset Apple Cake at the nearby cafe.

This is the recipe used on page 7.

DORSET APPLE CAKE

Dorset Apple Cake takes pride of place in an old fashioned English summer tea. Made with Bramley apples and topped with a sugar glaze it can be served either cold or warm with cream.

Cream together 225g each of butter and castor sugar. Add four large eggs and 250g of self-raising flour, alternately. Include 25g of cornflour. Fold into the mixture 225g of chopped Bramley apple. Pour into a cake tin 18cm in diameter. ~ Cut segments from an unpeeled apple and soak in lemon juice. Arrange in a circle round the top of the cake and dust with soft brown sugar to make a crusty glaze. ~ Bake at 170 C for about an hour and a quarter.

While Shaftesbury had a nunnery Sherborne had a monastery. It was a cathedral city in the days of the Saxon Kings. The monastery was established in 998. Its prosperity provided steady expansion in Saxon, Norman and Early English times. The dissolution in the 1530's put paid to the monastery but many of the buildings escaped un-damaged. The Monastic buildings behind the Abbey church are now the site of Sherborne school.

To the east of the town lie two castles, on either side of the river Yeo, which is dammed to make a lake. Sherborne Old Castle was built by the Bishop of Salisbury in the 12th century. It came into Sir Walter Raleigh's hands and he attempted to renovate it in the 1590's. Lacking a good DIY shop down the road he abandoned the struggle. Raleigh then built the New Sherborne Castle on the other side of the river. This curious building was expanded with polygonal turrets in 1600.

An apocryphal story is told about Raleigh in this house. One day he was smoking a pipe of tobacco, a newly discovered drug he had brought into England from the Americas.

A servant came in the room and saw him shrouded in smoke. Thinking that his master was on fire he threw a bucket of water over him!

Both castles were bought in 1616 by the Digby family after Sir Walter lost his head in the Tower of London.

The Old Castle survived a seige of 6,000 of Cromwell's men during the Civil War in 1642. Three years later Cromwell conducted another seige to get rid of "….this malicious mischievous Castle, like the owner." In this he succeeded.

Dorset is richly endowed with rivers. In times past there were many environmentaly friendly mills, using water to grind corn. The mill pond would contain trout for food. In some instances the river was used by boats to bring loads to and from the mill. The machinery at Sturminster Newton Mill still works. The trade now is in visitors.

Sherborne Abbey >

*W*ell, I've more trades than the beſt idle raſcal in all
England. I'm waiter and attend the company, as oſtler
I wait on horſes; I paints the names on the ſmugglers' boats;
I plays the fiddle at church; I'm, a tight lockſmith; I'm a bit'n a
pariſh conſtable; and for walking on meſſages to Weymouth,
Blandford, Corfe, Poole, or Wareham, I'm allow'd to be
as ſmart a footpad as any in the county of Dorſet.

JOHN O'KEEFFE 1793

BLACKMWORE MAIDENS

The primrwose in the sheade do blow,
The cowslip in the zun,
The thyme upon the down do grow,
The clote where streams do run;
An' where do pretty maidens grow
An' blow, but where the tow'r
Do rise among the bricken tuns,
In Blackmwore by the Stour.

WILLIAM BARNES 1801 - 1886

< *Old and New Sherborne Castles*
Monastery door >

*D*orset, is one of the most interesting and picturesque regions in the south-west of England. Still far behind the times as regards the modern stress and hurry of life, and even also as regards its thought and progress towards up-to-date modernity, it offers unique attractions for the student, archaeologist, and traveller of the old and truer type. The tourist of the more modern kind may perhaps find the district "slow," but of its picturesqueness, and not seldom romantic beauty, there can be no two opinions.

CLIVE HOLLAND 1906

A Dorset rustic, on being reproved by a magistrate for being drunk and disorderly, explained that his sad plight was the result of taking his liquor the wrong way up; for, said he,
"Cyder upon beer is very good cheer,
Beer 'pon cyder is a dalled bad rider!"

The worthy magistrate, not to be vanquished by the poetic tippler, told him to remember-
"When the cyder's in the can
The sense is in the man!
When the cyder's in the man
The sense is in the can."

R THURSTON HOPKINS 1922

< Gold Hill, Shaftesbury
Snow on Gold Hill >

T here is nothing special, in Britain, about living somewhere which has been lived in for a thousand years-indeed, in a kingdom so close-grained with human occupation it would be difficult not to do so,even in a suburb. Where the sense of continuity comes through with strong vibrations is, of course, if the house itself has been the home of trains of predecessors and has served a consistent purpose. To be included in the long, uncalled roll is a privilege which is both enhancing and humbling: you are merely another entry on that densely-layered palimpsest, and that is sufficient.

I write this near to a steady rush and thunder of water, but I have consciously to listen for it because it flows into the whole composition of the sounds of this small valley, and is euphonic. That is true in another way, too: the muffled roar comes from a river which long ago was pent in a culvert to supplement man's muscles by driving a wheel and, having been diverted to lend this extra power, the chalk stream from the adjacent escarpment is returned, unchanged and as fresh, to its parent race-a good way to work with nature.

KENNETH ALLSOP 1920 - 1973

< Sturminster Newton Mill
Country Signpost >

BOURNEMOUTH AND THE EAST

Wimborne Minster is like a grown up toy town. The old roads twist just slightly to give an interesting view whichever way you look. The double-towered Norman Minster Church once had a spire. This fell in 1600, in the middle of a service. No one was hurt, but it was thought provident not to replace the spire.

Into the 19th century the coast between Christchurch and Poole was a wild area where smugglers operated without fear. The first house was built in 1810. Fifty years later Bournemouth was still described as "a small collection of villas." A pine plantation made the town a pleasant place to walk and stroll. R L Stevenson came here because the mild climate was considered good for his tuberculosis. With the coming of the railway Bournemouth's expansion was speeded up. It grew to reach Poole in the west and Christchurch in the east. In 1972 Bournemouth and Christchurch were wrested from Hampshire and given to Dorset. The rest of Dorset was unsure about having a big metropolis handed to them. My feeling is that just as a symphony consists of loud and soft notes, the county of Dorset is enhanced by the contrast of a big city at its entrance.

Like many other places the priory at Christchurch has a legend that the building stones were mysteriously moved several times. This story is usually attached to places where pre-christian rituals took place. A monastery was established over 900 years ago. The town changed its name to Christchurch after a miracle during the building of the nave. A carpenter accidentally cut a huge beam too short. In the night the beam miraculously lengthened. A re-incarnation of Jesus Christ is said to be responsible! I don't believe it.

While taking the photograph of the Priory Church at dusk I was alone in the graveyard waiting for the correct light. I became aware of one or two people whispering behind me. I expected an amateur photographer to bore me about his camera or something. I turned round so that they knew I had heard them. THERE WAS NO ONE THERE! I nearly jumped out of my skin. For a few minutes I was aware of a ghost or two hiding behind gravestones. I left hurriedly.

Mudeford, on the eastern edge of the "new" expanded Dorset, is notable for the quay at the entrance to Christchurch harbour. With just a narrow gap the tidal waters rush with exceptionally strong currents.

As the river silted up at Wareham the port of Poole expanded. Some early travellers were surprised that Poole was so new, and undeveloped, until the early 17th century. Fine town houses were built in the 18th century when the profits of the "Newfoundland" trade were finally spent in the town. Unfortunately, many splendid houses were demolished in recent times. Only recently have the people of Poole preserved some of their heritage in the Old Town area.

Poole harbour is now a haven for small pleasure boats, cruisers and yachts. The largest island in the harbour is Brownsea. It has had a chequered history. Henry VIII used it as part of his coastal defences. Celia Fiennes describes in detail the extraction process for Copperas which was used in dyeing. After Copperas the island was used for clay extraction. The clay, however, was of poor quality and could only be used for drainage and sewer pipes. The pottery went bankrupt when it was discovered that the owner of the island had misused money belonging to the bank of which he was a director. When Baden Powell held his first, experimental Boy Scout Camp here in 1907 the island was owned by a multi-millionare, Mr van Raalte. After various kinds of mineral exploration it was, in hindsight, lucky that Mrs. Bonham-Christie bought the island in 1927. She lived an eccentric and reclusive life which meant that the island turned back into a wilderness. When the National Trust bought the island in 1961 it had become a valuable nature reserve. Today Brownsea Island is still being exploited for its mineral riches. The oil wells at Wytch Farm are driven at an angle, to tap the wealth under the island of which previous owners were unaware.

< *Tarrant Monkton*

*T*he Toun of Wimburn is yet meatly good and reasonably welle inhabitid. It hath bene a very large Thing, and was in price in tyme of the West-Saxon Kinges.

Ther be in and about it diverse Chapelles that in tymes past were chappeles to the toun.

LELAND 1540

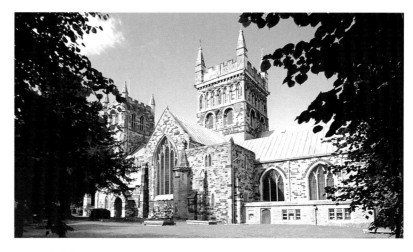

WIMBORNE

*T*he choire being then full of people at tenne of clock service, allsoe the streets by reason of the markett, a sudden mist ariseing, all the spire steeple, being of a very great height, was strangely cast down; the stones battered all the lead and brake much timber of the roofe of the church, yet without aine hurt to the people.

COKER 1600

< Wimborne from the air
Wimborne Minster >

I shall expire vulgarly at Bournemouth.

RUPERT BROOKE 1907

I was just 18 and on my holidays. My younger brother aged 12, and a cousin aged 14, proposed to chase me. After I had been hunted for twenty minutes and was rather short of breath, I decided to cross the bridge. Arrived at its centre I saw to my consternation that the pursuers had divided their forces. One stood at each end of the bridge; capture seemed certain. But in a flash there came across me a great project. The chine which the bridge spanned was full of young fir trees. Their slender tops reached to the level of the footway. "Would it not" I asked myself "be possible to leap on to one of them and slip down the pole-like stem, breaking off each tier of branches as one descended, until the fall was broken?" I looked at it. I computed it. I meditated. Meanwhile I climbed over the balustrade. My young pursuers stood wonderstruck at either end of the bridge. To plunge or not to plunge, that was the question! In a second I had plunged, throwing out my arms to embrace the summit of the fir tree. The argument was correct; the data were absolutely wrong. It was three days before I regained consciousness and more than three months before I crawled from my bed.

WINSTON CHURCHILL 1892

Bournemouth Pier >
< Bournemouth Beach

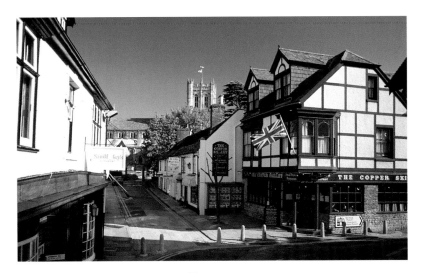

*I felt a sudden tenderness for Bournemouth, for all the old
people in Bath chairs, for the discreet gardens and the
shaven lawns and the tulips and the town clerk, the mayor
and the corporation, even for old colonels with enlarged livers
in enlarged check suits, and for all the bored married people
of whom the hotels are full...*

H V MORTON 1927

*My first was to Bournemouth, where I was engaged after
Easter, for six months to teach French and the dead
languages, by Mr. Remington, a Protestant clergyman who had
been converted to Catholicism, at his small but very select school of
St. Aloysius (St Louis of Gonzaga). The house built like a chalet,
looked over the sea, but from a distance, so that we could only see
its extreme horizon. The scarcely perceptible "white horse", the
shining sails of the fishing boats, and the red smoke of the steamers
as they were on the point of disappearing or were just gone out of
sight. The town is what is called on the other side of the Channel,
a "watering place"; pretty, quiet, without any trade, a beach with
no port, but with a jetty for form's sake, surrounded by charming
woods in which the pine predominates. I took my boys down to the
beach every day and bathed with them. They were not numerous,
an average of a dozen at the outside, of whom some were Irish and
these were real imps.*

PAUL VERLAINE JULY 1894

Priory Church, Christchurch >
< Christchurch

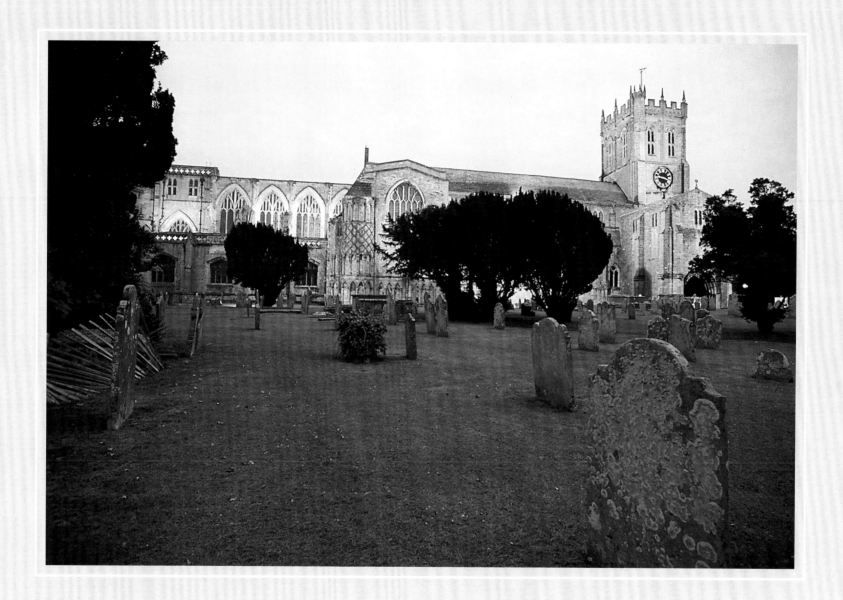

"Would you," she said, "like a lobster?"

I observed her closely and realized that she was serious. Behind her lay in negligent attitudes dozens of lobsters on a table among roses. It was 4.30 p.m. It had never occurred to me that people eat lobster at tea-time. In fact, there is to my mind something almost indecent about it. I was so embarrassed that I said "Yes", whereupon, giving me no time to repent, in the manner of women, she picked up a big scarlet brute and disappeared, leaving me to slink miserably to a chintz chair, with a clammy foreboding of great evil.

"Tea?" she asked. I made a feeble protest, but she assured me that China tea 'goes' with lobster. I wanted to ask whether this experiment had ever been tried before by man, but I was given no time. When the shell was empty some devil entered into me and urged me to reply "Yes" to everything this girl said (and she was a good talker), with the result that basins of Dorset cream, pots of jam, puffy cakes oozing sweetness, ramparts of buns and crisp rolls became piled up behind the rose-bowl. The only thing I missed at this tea-party was the Mad Hatter. We of London hear stories of West Country excesses: of creamy dawns and jammy eyes. Was this, I reflected, an unofficial welcome to Dorset.

H V MORTON 1927

< Mudeford
Mudeford Beach >

South of this Town, over a Sandy wild and barren Country, we came to Pool, a conſiderable Sea-Port, indeed the moſt conſiderable in all this Part of England; for here I found ſome Ships, ſome Merchants, and ſome Trade; eſpecially, here were a good Number of Ships fitted out every Year to the Newfoundland Fiſhing, in which the Pool Men were ſaid to have been particularly Succeſsful for many Years paſt.

DANIEL DEFOE 1724

Westward the sands by storm and drift have gained
A barrier, and that barrier maintained,
Backed by a sandy heath, whose deep-worn road
Deny'd the groaning wagon's ponderous load,
This branches southwards at the point of Thule,
Forms the harbour of the town of Poole.

WILLIAM TURNER 1811

Old Poole Town >
< The Old Customs House

*F*rom thence by boate we went to a little Isle called Brownsea 3 or 4 leagues off, where there is much Copperice made, the stones being found about the Isle in the shore in great quantetyes, there is only one house there which is the Governours, besides little fishermens houses they being all taken up about the Copperice wokes; they gather the stones and place them on the ground raised like the beds in gardens, rows one above the other, and are all shelving so that the raine disolves the stones and it drains down into trenches and pipes made to receive and convey it to the house; that is fitted with iron panns foursquare and of a pretty depth at least 12 yards over, they place iron spikes in the panns full of branches and so as the liquor boyles to a candy it hangs on those branches: I saw some taken up it look't like a vast bunch of grapes, the coullour of the Copperace not being much differing, it lookes cleare like suger-candy.

CELIA FIENNES 1690

*R*ound the (first Scout) camp fire the Chief told us thrilling yarns, himself led the Eengonyama chorus and in his inimitable way held the attention and won the hearts of all. I can see him still, as he stands in the flickering light - an alert figure, full of the joy of life, now grave, now gay, answering all manner of questions, imitating the call of birds, showing how to stalk a wild animal, flashing out a little story, dancing and singing round the fire, pointing a moral, not in actual words, but in such an elusive yet convincing way that everyone present, boy or man, was ready to follow him, wherever he might lead.

P W EVERETT 1957

< *Brownsea Island*
Sandbanks >

ISLE OF PURBECK

The Isle of Purbeck is not much of an island. It's not even much of a peninsula. In the past things were slightly different. Before modern roads the heathland was mostly impenetrable. Early books recount that a guide was necessary to avoid getting lost. Last year, while taking photographs near the Agglestone, I took what looked to be a well-worn path. Within a few yards the path gave way. The sandy path turned to quicksand. I escaped with very muddy boots.

The bridge at Wareham was the best way to access the Purbeck downs. Until the river Frome silted up Wareham was a busy port. As a harbour Poole was developed only when Wareham's fortunes faded. Crossing the river by the fine mediaeval bridge made Purbeck a remote and special place.

Studland Beach is the newest part of Dorset. Sea currents have added sand to the small promontory which almost closes Poole harbour. The beach at Shell Bay, on which many small shells are washed ashore, stretches from South Haven Point, opposite Sandbanks, all the way to Studland village. This two and a half mile stretch of lonely sand is deserted for most of the year. When summer comes the chain link ferry brings thousands of holiday makers from Poole and Bournemouth.

Inland from the beach lies the nature reserve of Studland Heath. Once considered a worthless stretch of poor sandy soil it is now seen as a valuable site for wild birds. The only structure of any size is the production platform bringing up valuable oil from deep underground. A curiosity on a small sandy hill is the Agglestone. Legend has an account of the Devil on the Isle of Wight. One night he hurled a rock at Corfe Castle but fortunately missed. Other stories have it as a meteorite. In reality it is simply a piece of natural sandstone and a graffiti target for anyone who ever loved Tracy, Shaun, Debbie or Gary.

A stronger link with the Isle of Wight can be seen at Handfast Point and Old Harry Rocks. These high chalk cliffs were once connected to The Needles. Erosion by the sea has gradually shaped the coastline to what we know today. In future years the coast will change again as the erosion continues. Until a hundred years ago Old Harry had a neighbouring stack called Old Harry's Wife who was washed away in a storm.

Another dramatic example of sea erosion is Lulworth Cove, which just borders the Isle of Purbeck. On either side of the Cove the contorted strata of limestone can be seen. When the sea found an opening it created a fine oval harbour in the softer stone behind.

A second geological wonder is a short way west, along the coastal path. Durdle Door is a natural stone arch in the sea. This too is doomed to erode and collapse.

The quarries of Purbeck were mined extensively for building stone. In places the cliffs themselves were cut up and shipped away. The quarry workings also created man-made harbours. Here boats would load up direct from the cliff face. Tilly Whim Caves and Dancing Ledge are examples of this. These cliff-side harbours were extremely hazardous and only used in fine summer weather. In winter, and for inland quarries, Swanage was used. Situated in a fine sheltered beach the harbour was busy for many years.

John Mowlem and his nephew, George Burt, were the major suppliers of Purbeck stone in London. They used a variety of interesting items as ballast on their ships return journeys. The result is that Swanage has a mish-mash of buildings, a clock-tower, bollards and lamposts from London.

Like a volcano standing in a gap in the chalk ridge the site for Corfe Castle was one of the best defended castles in the realm. In 978 King Edward was murdered here by his stepmother's men. Elfrida's, son, Ethelred, then succeeded to the English throne.

In 1646 the Royalists held the castle against Cromwell's men. On May Day in 1643 it was a traditional day for stag-hunting. While the mayor and local gentry were out hunting, Cromwell's men laid siege to Corfe Castle. A technique that hunt saboteurs of today would relish. Lady Bankes held the castle for the Royalists for nearly three years. When the Parlimentarians finally took the castle it was with inside help. Parliament ordered that the castle be destroyed.

Purbeck Stile >

The Agglestone is a heavy mass of eroded sandstone fixed on the summit of a rounded hill and dominating the heathland. It is the subject of the usual tiresome legends concerning the Devil, who is supposed to have thrown it at someone or something and, as usual, misjudged the distance.

PAUL NASH 1935

A section of the beach to the north of Studland has been designated a zone where naturists can roam without embarrassment - embarrassment, that is, for those people who keep their clothes on. To one side of a notice, ladies and gentlemen sit in deck chairs. They change with towels wrapped tightly around them and get their nudity from the tabloid newspapers. To the other side of the notice, naturists sit on rafia mats. Pubic diamonds, little bald willies and bosoms of every shape, size and colour abound. Everyone is happy and free and reads the Guardian. It was into this latter section that Boogie wandered, stating clearly which side of the fence his political interests lie.

MARK WALLINGTON 1982

Agglestone Rock >
< Shell Beach, Studland

"Her was a clever woman; her kept my things straight," he said to me one night at supper, as he looked wistfully at his old jacket full of simple rents from hedgerow briars. "But it's no manner of use grumbling - I never was a bull-sowerlugs (a morose fellow). And thank the Lord she was took quick. I went off for the doctor four miles away, and when I gets there he was gone off somewhere else; so I turned, and in tramping back along remembered I had a bottle of medicine which he did give me last year, so says I, "That will do for the ol' woman"; so I gave it to her and she died."

The old blacksmith drank his beer and dealt with his ham and bread for ten minutes in silence. Then he looked into the amber depths of his ale and said: "Say, mister - wasn't it a good job I didn't take that bottle of physic myself?"

R THURSTON HOPKINS 1922

< Old Harry Rocks
Handfast Point >

"At length I am escaped from the world's greatest snare. This is heaven. Downs, hens, cottages and the sun. All morning I souse myself in Elizabethan plays; and every afternoon I walk up perpendicular places alone for hours".

RUPERT BROOKE 1910

*B*y the time that we had fully ſurveyed the Cove, the day cloſed, and the moon beginning to ſhed a beautiful luſtre on the ſurface of the waves, preſented us with a truly delightful ſpectacle. The tide gently rippled againſt the rocks, the broad white foreheads of which reflected large maſſes of light, and formed a fine contraſt to the gloom of the overſhadowed ſea in the Cove; - the heavens were ſerene; - not a whiſper of wind was heard; - and, in ſhort, the beauty of the whole ſcene was ſo uncommonly exquiſite that it ſeemed to have been raiſed by enchantment. We quitted this ſpot with reluctance, and not without many a pauſe to take a farewell peep at it.

WILLIAM GEORGE MATON M.A. 1797

Lulworth Cove from the air >
< *Lulworth Cove*

I doubt if there be around England a more picturesque stretch of coast, for its length, than that which borders the sea from Swanage to Weymouth. Certainly there is no shore which presents so many contrasts and variations in so few pleasant miles. In this sea line are cliffs of jagged rocks, sheer as a bastion wall, as well as green lawns which creep lazily to the water's edge. There are wide, open bays, and fissured sea-echoing chines. There are round coves, inlets reached through archedrocks, level sands, and moaning caves. There are beaches of shingle, of pebbles, of colossal boulders, and the clay of crumbling banks; precipices of every colour, from the white of chalk to the black of the shale; and walls of stone streaked with tints of yellow, buff or red.

FREDERICK TREVES 1906

< Durdle Door >

When I returned to the Cove Tavern for my knapsack, the landlord tried to dissuade me from travelling along the cliffs, it was "such rough walking," nothing but ups and downs, with risk of falling, and so forth-all of which might be avoided by taking the road "inside the hills," as he expressed it. For rough walking my mind was made up; and for the rest, I doubted not that where a coast-guard man could walk, I could walk also Moreover, I had come to see the cliffs with all their variety of form and outline, and the glorious expanse of sea beyond. But I was advised so many times to take an inland route, as to make me suspect at last the existence of a wish to keep strangers away from the cliffs.

WALTER WHITE 1825

The sun and wind made the long grass flicker like fire on the Kimmeridge Ledges. I walked these cliffs through the hot afternoon and did not meet another soul. There were pastures on the cliffs, and just to the left of the overgrown path two hundred vertical feet of gull-clawed air to the sliding surf and the whole ocean beyond. This was the most beautiful stretch of coast I had seen so far, and I was alone on it. My happiness was greatly increased by the thought that I did not have the slightest idea where I was going. I always felt I was safe - everything would be fine - if I stayed on the coast.

PAUL THEROUX 1982

Baits Head Sunset >
< Strip Lynchets

I can gather no otherwife, but wheras of old tymes Shippes cam fumwhat nere Wereham up the Haven, and there had vente of their Wares, and fynnes Shippes loft their Rode ther for lak of Depth of Water Shippes kept and refortid nerer to Pole Toun, aud fo it by a litle encreafid, and Wareham felle clene to ruines. Howbeit Wareham was ons fore rafid in the Danes Warres.

JOHN LELAND 1540

Y ou wonder what I am doing? Well, so do I, in truth. Days seem to dawn, suns to shine, evenings to follow, and then I sleep. What I have done, what I am doing, what I am going to do, puzzle me and bewilder me. Have you ever been a leaf and fallen from your tree in autumn and been really puzzled by it? That's the feeling.

T E LAWRENCE 6 May 1935

< Wareham
Wareham at night >

S WANWICH is fituated in a very low fpot, but it enjoys a pleafing fea- fcene, bounded by Peverel-point, on one fide, and Studland- foreland on the other. The bay is extremely commodious for the bathing machine, and, of courfe, attracts a few families to the town in the watering feafon. A great quantity of ftone is fhipped from the quay, and previoufly cut into convenient maffes for paving and building. We were informed that nearly fifty thoufand tons are put on board annually, the beft fort felling for twelve fhillings per ton at the veffel.

WILLIAM GEORGE MATON 1797

T he Halsewell struck on the rocks at a part of the shore where the cliff is of vast height, and rises almost perpendicular from its base. But at this particular spot, the foot of the cliff is excavated into a cavern of ten or twelve yards in depth, and of breadth equal to the length of a large ship. The sides of the cavern are so nearly upright as to be difficult of access; and the bottom is strewn with sharp and uneven rocks, which seem by some convulsion of the earth to have been detached from its roof.

The ship lay with her broadside opposite to the mouth of this cavern, with her whole length stretched almost from side to side of it. But when she struck, it was too dark for the unfortunate persons on board to discover the real magnitude of the danger, and the extreme horror of such a situation.

< Dancing Ledge
Swanage >

CHARLES DICKENS 1853

89

The historical part of the guide-book is admirably written, but my fellow pilgrims grudged the necessary sixpence to buy it. They bought the picture-postcards instead. It amused me to hang about, overhearing scraps of small talk:

"Oh, look, dear, what pretty baa-lambs!"

"I could do with a cooler, I could."

"Must 'ave 'ad an earthquake here, I'd say."

"Don't you go near them old ruins; all of a topple they are."

"Why do we have to pay a tanner to get in here?"

Thoughtfully, the present owner, a Bankes of Kingston Lacy, has put up a notice disclaiming any responsibility if the ruins do topple over. Listening to the talk of trippers one wonders why they do not.

HORACE ANNESLEY VACHELL 1861-1955

Till lately Corfe has been out of the beaten tourist track, but now the railway has found it out, and who knows how long it will retain its primitive picturesqueness? Fortunately there are no large cities or towns near that breed the noisy tripper, for when he invades a spot there is a truce to all romancing, and the luxury of a little harmless day-dreaming becomes an impossibility.

JAMES JOHN HISSEY 1896

Corfe Castle Village >
< Corfe Castle

90

*O*ne of these porticoed houses is the Greyhound-a modest
hostelry, but possessed of satisfactory capabilities as regards
the commissariat. A quiet breakfast at a little country inn is not
the least among the enjoyments of travel. The unadulterated milk,
the really new-laid eggs, the sweet, fresh butter, all inspire a
confidence unfelt in cities, and you eat with unwonted satisfaction.

WALTER WHITE 1825

*T*he time has come for us to bid our readers
adieu. We have, as it were, traversed in
company the length and breadth of the county,
peeped at its past glories, admired its present
beauties. No county is there in England more
fondly enshrined in the hearts of her sons; no
tract of country so deserving of their affection. In
a word, Dorset is a thing of beauty and a joy for
ever.

MAJOR H.O.LOCK 1925

< The Greyhound Inn, Corfe Castle
Corfe Castle from a distance >

PHOTOGRAPHY NOTES

This collection of photographs spans a period of eleven years. Although I return several times to some locations I always find something different. Weather is a constant factor in landscape photography. Camping on the ridge above Abbotsbury, I once spent five days waiting for the rain to stop. In those days I was too broke to go home and come back another day. I practised taking pictures using a compass to decide where the sun should be. On the sixth day dawn brought broken sunshine. I dashed from location to location setting up my camera in my pre-planned places. When it was time for breakfast I had made seven pictures!

A mystery. Several years ago I planned a picture on Charmouth Beach. I knew that the light would be right at about seven thirty in the morning. I went to reconnoitre the site the evening before. About every twenty yards down the beach sat an angler. Judging by their hurricane lamps and picnic boxes they would be there all night. According to my tide-table the high tide was due at about mid night. I started chatting to one of the fishermen. It was an angling competition. They were fishing all night until seven in the morning. I asked if he knew anything about the tides. "The organisers have sorted out the tides, they don't reach this far," he told me.

Before dawn the next morning I pulled into the car park. I had borrowed a rock with embedded fossils from Mr Langdon's Fossil Shop in Lyme Regis. With this weighty rock in a rucksack on my back and my camera case over my shoulder I started walking down the beach. Just in case the anglers had left behind a pile of maggots on the spot I carried a bucket to wash them away. I also carried a broom to sweep away footprints and a camera tripod. It was still a few minutes before the competition was due to end. I expected to see fishing rods busy, hoping to catch that last minute sea bass. Instead the beach was empty. I had the whole place to myself. Not a footprint to be seen. No maggots or litter at the base of the cliffs. There was ample evidence that the tide had reached right up to the base of the cliff and beyond.

I never did find out what happened to the angling club secretary when over a hundred fishermen had to abandon the beach at midnight!

· ·

Also In this series -

From Cornwall With Love
Photographs by Bob Croxford

ISBN 0952185008

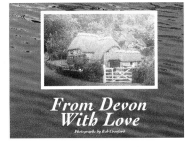

From Devon With Love
Photographs by Bob Croxford

ISBN 0952185016

From Bath With Love

ISBN 0952185024

From The Cotswolds With Love
Photographs by Bob Croxford

ISBN 0952185040

INDEX

Entries including photographs are in BOLD type. Those properties which include National Trust Properties are marked with an *.

WRITERS

ACKNOWLEDGEMENTS

This is now my fourth book in a series. Julie Simmonds has again provided valuable help with the donkey work of typing, filing etc.. She also administers the more complex bits with rare efficiency and hard work.

When compiling an anthology there is often a point when the collection of quotes reaches critical mass. With this collection that point was reached on finding Rodney Legg's LITERARY DORSET. Not only is it an invaluable source of who wrote what in Dorset, its a good read as well. Desmond Hawkins' WESSEX, A LITERARY CELEBRATION offered other useful pointers. Jo Draper's DORSET is the invaluable complete guide to places. The GOLDENEYE Pictorial Guide and Map is a good way to find your way around Dorset and has most useful opening times and other data.

Thanks to the staff at Dorchester and Bournemouth reference libraries who dealt patiently with my requests.

The quotation from FIVE HUNDRED MILE WALKIES by Mark Wallington is reproduced by kind permission of Hutchinson Publishers.

The quotations from A TRAGEDY OF TWO AMBITIONS and THE TRUMPET MAJOR by Thomas Hardy are reproduced with kind permission of Macmillan General Books.

The quotation from THE SHELL GUIDE 1935 by Paul Nash is reproduced by kind permission of Shell UK.

The quotation from A WRITER'S DIARY by Virginia Woolf edited by Leonard Woolf is reproduced by kind permission of The Estate of Virginia Woolf, the Estate of the Editor and Chatto & Windus Publishers.

The quotation from the poem POOR HONEST MEN in RUDYARD KIPLING'S VERSE:DEFINITIVE EDITION by Rudyard Kipling is reproduced by kind permission of A P Watt Ltd on behalf of The National Trust For Places of Historic Interest or Natural Beauty.

The poem WAGTAIL AND BABY by Thomas Hardy is reproduced with permission of Papermac Books.

The quotation from MY VAGABONDAGE by Horace Annesley Vachell is reproduced by permission of Mrs J L Dennis.

The quotation from A KINGDOM BY THE SEA by Paul Theroux © 1983 is reproduced by permission of Hamish Hamilton Ltd.

The quotation from IN THE COUNTRY by Kenneth Allsop is reproduced by permission of Peters Fraser & Dunlop Group Ltd.

The poem DORSET from COLLECTED POEMS by John Betjeman is reproduced by permission of John Murray (Publishers) Ltd.

The quotations from WEYMOUTH SANDS and WOLF SOLENT by John Cowper Powys are reproduced by permission of the Estate of John Cowper Powys.

The quotation from MY EARLY LIFE by Winston S Churchill is reproduced by permission of Curtis Brown Ltd. London on behalf of The Estate of Sir Winston S. Churchill, 1930.

The quotation from BRITAIN BESIDE THE SEA by Christopher Somerville © 1989 published by Grafton Books is reproduced by permission of Richard Scott Simon Ltd.

The quotation from THE LETTERS OF T E LAWRENCE is reproduced by permission of the Trustees of the Seven Pillars of Wisdom Trust.

The quotation from IN SEARCH OF ENGLAND by H V Morton published by Methuen London Ltd is reproduced by permission of Reed Books on behalf of the Estate of H V Morton.

The quotations from A FRENCH LIEUTENANT'S WOMAN by John Fowles are reproduced by kind permission of the author.